About the Author

K.B. Ludlow writes stories and poems.

The Poppy in the Black of the Gothic Night is a collection of poems that can be best described as going on a journey through the surreal, the dark, the martial and the romantic.

He enjoys words and reading poets. Two of his favourites are Emily Dickinson and Edgar Allan Poe, as well as Keats, Shelley and Samuel Taylor Coleridge.

K.B. Ludlow writes in South Australia – his favourite place to live!

Dedicated to Mabel.

K. B. Ludlow

Pretty Flowers in the Snow

AUSTIN MACAULEY PUBLISHERS™

LONDON • CAMBRIDGE • NEW YORK • SHARJAH

A CIP catalogue record for this title is available from the British Library.

ISBN 9781398481039 (Paperback)
ISBN 9781398481046 (ePub e-book)

www.austinmacauley.com

First Published 2023
Austin Macauley Publishers Ltd
1 Canada Square
Canary Wharf
London
E14 5AA

Acknowledgements

A special acknowledgement is due to Tara Douglas for her input into the last ten poems, especially 'Whales'.

I would also like to acknowledge my family for their encouragement, feedback and support for the 'Poppy' trilogy.

POEMS

In the Glow of the Red

Cemetery walls
Man made waterfalls
Roses
The hand of beautiful death
Grass fields,
Tainted red
In the glow of the red
Statue of Mother Mary, cascaded moon
All dead
Headstone in pounding silence
Congregation meets
Soon for them
Death will greet

Caffeine

The Frankenstein calls his monster
Caffeine-fuelled world
Darkness stars of time
Chemical disturbing
Unwind
Sensory deprivation, in the brains
Caffeine veins
A muse
A quiet friend
The end
Words of inspiration
To the hand that holds the pen

Ghost at the Piano

Ash black
Lace wearing swan
Arms outstretched
She looks my way
Sheet music etched
Luminous black suit
Cascaded by blonde hair
Streaks of ruby blond
Mesmerized by her stare
A grey swan
Disturbing beauty
Hypnotic spider fingers
She is my inner hell
Sweet succulent delight
Is she a ghost…or have I lost my sight?
Beauty like a washed-out painting

Alien Spy Catcher

Greetings Earthlings
Welcome from Mars
I go to space to visit the stars
Spies have infiltrated everywhere
I catch them with my gun
I was the one who created the sun

I fly in my UFO
It's a Porsche
I even listen to music
Called Black Orchid
I am the lead guitarist
So, we can rock the universe
On stage

Greetings Earthlings
Welcome from mars
I go to space to visit the stars
Spies have infiltrated everywhere
I catch them with my gun
I am the one who invented the sun

Haemoglobin

The angels said goodbye
I dreamed
Floating on a boat
On a river of angel tears
I rowed down that stream
Listening to those screams
Flying in a caged wall of razors

A Song for the Broken Hearted

I dreamed of you
Your tender kiss
There you were
Holding the hand
Of the one you had given your heart to

The Coma of God

Pray to God
Is he on life support?
'Cause he's not listening
Left in a hospital ward linked to machines
Dreaming
About all the worlds he creates
And planet Earth
Man, he's one mistake

To Our Passing Loved Ones

It's cruel that we grow old
That to death our soul is sold
And cruel that some die young
And soldiers' battle-cries
Unsung
We watch and weep and cry
But your time slips us by
To the age of nothingness
No angels here to bless

Dark matter... The Decay in the Light

Sleep
No one hears me scream
Death is my companion
When I fall to dream
Like a cloak of black
The cloak eclipses time
Waiting for my companion
To bring to the light
I see
The decay in the light
This inner struggle
I see death in sight
Fire friendly angels
Summon death
My friend death takes me in the night
Surreal beauty
I see with sight

The Tiger Unleased

No inner peace
Sleepers and Valium
Intoxication increased

All she sees is despair
Surrounded in bottle syringe walls
Concrete walls
Trees and a train go by
She falls in the dark

Snow on a grave
No name
Homelessness

Moonbeam of Roses

There's a light beam
A spotlight
And a dying star
She dreams of silver screens
Sleeping under a bridge
Shut out by the world
Now in a fridge
Roses fall, with glowing snow
Upon a headstone
20 below
I look into the mirror
A reincarnated past
Beauty,
Stillness
Wanting it to last

Hear the Cries of Appeal

When the black crow cometh
Hear the cries of appeal
When the grave revealed
Vanishing time etched on a crow's beak
Standing in the shadow
Death does speak
Within the shadow
Like a good friend

Standing in the Shadows

Darkness comes to me
Within the crow's shadow
Like a common friend
That's been missing
Death reminiscing
On all the souls
Sleepy souls,
Four walls begin to
Shake
Shake
Quake

FEAR!

Fear of death touching me
Lurking in the shadows
We all walk
The long, long halls
Towards the gallows
Death touch
Chills! The agony and ecstasy
Of death
DYING!
With awaited breath
REFLECT!
On the divine
Before the abyss creeps
Eternal sleep

Mars Imagined

Like the flamingo on a salted lake
Death creeping, awake
No oxygen planetary star horizon
Rockets arising in the silence of black eternity
No Martians
No water
No trees
Dust and wind
Like red bees in the air

Smoking Poem

The light up
The orange, red glow
White paper like snow
The words grey on the page
As the flame hugs the page
Twisting!
Turning!
Oblivion!
Burning!
Smoke, the hand of death.
Taking words
Taking breath
Warm, hot
Crumbling into snow powder

Thought Turn to Ash

The sun melts to liquid
My heart is torn apart
Now the blood had ruptured
I dreamed of you
When I was young
Misery kept me well
Now I await
In a cocoon of my inner hell
Like petals falling

The Darkness Falls

The darkness falls
Upon the trench
Time to clear the bodies
The stench

Enemy advance
Enemy advance
Towards carols sung
The peace of silent night
Has begun

The Band Who Summoned Death

By the lake
Above the moon
The band begin to play
For coming doom
I sat and mourned
When darkness fell
Like a radiation winter
I saw her cloak of despair

A Trip down Memory Jane

In the mirror
Death drawing nearer
Her fucking voice,
I still fuckin hear her
The reflection deep
Crack glass on the floor
Cold quicksilver black
Cannot find the door
My stem liquid blood
Runs deep down the arm
Like a violent storm
No one sees the calm
And I'm calm
As the lady arrives
Can't believe she's death
So, touches me, just barely alive
Falling through the floor
The mirror fragments
I grab the door
But it's too late
I see my ancestors
Another pill
My brain wilts
Spine chills
The darkness inside
Is there anything keeping it alive
Can't hold back
From the brave
Cut too deep
Now in a grave
I feel the dark

Eve Shattered

Hugging herself
In a crimson shower
Water stains of red
Death awaking to devour
Steam from hot water
Outside the bleakest moon
Death greets her warm

It's still outside
Like the eye of a tornado
Candle like a live spirit dancing
As she awaits to die

Shadows lurk
Like the paparazzi
A reckless tyrant forms
Shadows on the wall
No longer in the calm
Before the storm

Death Hold a Red Rose

As the wind does blow
And all I see is death
Warmed by his, invisible breath

Writing a song
Treble clef
A dark solemn tune
That matches my impending doom

The Darkness of Life

Welcome
Come inside
Where darkness lurks
In the human mind
Time ticks
Those sorrowful minutes
Suicide
Within its
Reach
Learning too late
Mortal enemy is its own sword
When the act is raised
Against the lord
But what kind of God
Would consider that to be a sin
Tell me lord
If you're in………

ATM

Welcome, may I help you
The concierge said
The line out the door
One teller on the floor
ATMs
Ready to rise up and take over
CEO of the bank earning millions
While they can only afford one teller
And close branches

Alien Fugitive

Alien
Alien
Invading aerospace
Intergalactic
Intelligent race
Done with nuclear war
Now superior lasers
Hangar 18
Try and invade us
Anal probe to see how a human works
In my spacecraft
Unidentified flying object
Can't see me with my ray gun
Clock of invisibility
Up to my planet something gone wrong
I accidentally blew up
The Pentagon
Alien
Alien

America

Give me the American dream
Protests
Burning cars in the street
Rich becoming richer
Poor becoming poorer
Hollywood
Blood
Actress on the floor
Guns shooting lives 200 rounds
People screaming
Lying dead on the ground
Coronavirus
Highest death count of a progressed nation
Where's the sense in it all
There's no explanation
Presidents busy tweeting
Procrastination
While lives die
In this great nation

A Robot Hamlet

Circuitry haywire
Fully aware
Virus on the world
Technology despair
Skull in my hand
Whisper from a white curtain
To be or not to be…that is the question?
Nuke the world
Recreate the world in a robot's image

Stars Started to Rain

Blackest beauty
Full lit moon
Space station planets
Gravity keeps me grounded
Magnetic rays from the sun
Streaks of light burning through the atmosphere
Like a Millennium Falcon in light speed

Light Illuminating the Cold Dark Decay of Life

Balancing Covid-19 with a subtle knife
Twisting and morphing
The shadows twist
Twisting and morphing
Like death is a contortionist
Grave of sorrow
As a VIRUS takes flight
The world still positive
When there's no end of death in sight

The Ghost of Keats

With a pen in hand
Composing poems
Like the ghost of Keats
On a stormy night
Looking out the window
A ghost composes a hallow tune
Like a child genius sponge
In the mansion…Dancing ghost and empty halls

Took My Hand

And showed me the light
From all
That had taken life
Walking in an unconfident man
Rising
Pull me through the ashes

Now I look at the words you gave me
Unleashed from my heart
It seems to me
That life is just about to start

Black Rose

On a thornless stem
Surrounded by red
A swan's beak
A black oblivion
Decaying surrounds the beauty
Laid on a coffin
Steel wood and mortal clay

You will wilt and die
Like the one inside who passes
To be buried light suffocate
Under soil and grass

Life flourished
After death
For mother earth
And all who blessed

Treasure the moments we have left
Life is so fleeting
Success bittersweet
When your time is up
And death comes to your street

Knocking on the door
Your soul leaves
And you engage in battle
But please no plead
For an hour
Will give you inner peace
Appreciate life before you are deceased

Death Played the Guitar

Got my six-string acoustic
Hand it to death
He got magic fingers
On his left
Strumming away
He plays a solemn tune
Looks out the window
Rains wilts the rose in June
He's playing a diminished chord
He's nearly finished
By the end my spirit rises
Caged for a moment
Pale gold light
By the fifteenth-century mirror
An American Gothic
She called to me
'Take my hand…I'll set you free'

Suicide Silique

Too many hills
Too many pills
He sits in my room
Is my fate sealed
Praying on the time that I have left
Not ready to enter those hallowed halls yet
White ceilings…white walls
No one knows the pain to befall
I call
Doctors call and machine stops beeping…
Through the wall.
Light at the end of the dark hall
No not yet…. not ready to fall…and enter that hall

Heroin Tears

Unconscious
Silver teaspoon mirror
Paramedic
Lake's reflection
Clouded veins
Blackbird touches
Red train track up an arm
Silky skin…an angel's lips
Kiss the spoon…needle
Overdose
Heavenly trip
Needle left on a sun-bleached sand
Devil wakes as children…bare feet
God at the wheel falling to sleep

Can't Hug a Memory 2

Innocence
Before death was real
Sitting in a lounge
Without a care
As Grandma died
On a bus
Bus warp slow motion
In the dark
The light finally came
Began to rain
Like a shit storm
Life in vain
No more hugs
Voice in a grave
Her genetics in my hand print
See her in a reflection
See her in a dream
But you can't hug a memory

Ghost from the Grave

Shooting stars
Crystals twinkling in the night
Something out there that fright
Like a ghost in chains
Take neither life nor death
Can't bare the totality of it all
Their final breath

Time

The end
Mortal pages I grow tired
Saw pain
When gazed into family's eyes
Weary I am not
Will not expire
These solemn poems
Like the murals on the walls

A Trip down Memory Jane 2

I was young
You were crazy
Insane
You thought my brain was lazy
And I was in hysterics
You were abusive
Your authority…misused it
I grew up
But that wounded child won't heal

Writer's Block 1

There's a suburb
Where words don't go
It comes and goes
And makes you slow
I take a chance with the paper
Like a razor romance
My pen my weapon of defence
When nothing make sense
The fog clears
My arsenal attacks
My words flow
Spontaneous

You Visited Me in the Dark

The storm of beauty
Talked to me in my darkest hour
Which was really my poetic muse
Now I've lost you
I'm so confused
Like a blood stain
You left a trace of DNA in my heart
But your just about to start
Take these mummified bandages off the wall
Let the ceiling cave in
Bring back the light

Summer Rain

Fireball blisters the earth
Clouds roll in on the horizon
The evening enters
The wind blows beneath the trees
Spots of water
Bring back fond memories
Rain scatters
And cools the hot scorched skin
Scented aurora from hot wet bitumen

Hopscotch

To a dark episode
The struggle within
Skin and water
Jane burns at the stake
Asleep
In the room next door
Shot dead
On the floor
A puppet
Cut the strings
Playing hopscotch
Jumping inside fractured squares
Shadows real but not there
In the sky
Roses on the stage
Curtain razed
Applaud
Curtain close
Encore

In a Grave

Shadow
You said you would keep in touch
You didn't
Pay phone and letters
Married to the world
And grave beyond
How come?
Tough times weren't there
Things go wrong
Shoot for the moon
Shoot for the stars
Satellite

A Daughter Named?

She has fond memories with her name
Made no mistakes
They walked through the park
Tree swings
Until it was getting dark
They had doll and tree house parties
She hugged away the pain
Now
She can't remember her name
If she had a daughter
She would name her Jane
Flashes of weddings grandchildren
But now sits in chair
Doesn't remember
This is the cruel life of dementia

My Friend Saw Santa the Other Day

My friend saw Santa and revealed his rear end
Blinded by the light
Santa said 'be my sleigh guide tonight'
Rudolph trapped with Covid restrictions
He has to quarantine
Not nostalgic about the past
And there's a planet
Named after an arse
Uranus
They've got Covid too
Santa caught it
Now he's in the poo

Junkie at the Train Station

Taste the spoon
Under the moon
Under the burning flame
Addiction can't contain
Train track riding up the arm
Needle danger
Disarm
Blood and brown sugar mix
Always searching for their next fix

The Darkness Rises

He tries to break out
But he flakes out, like dandruff in a hair
Seems that 20 years
He's prayers
Have fallen on deaf ears
Flippin the bird
Struggle with the words
And angelic rose
Asks
Is he a god?
Angel augmented
Feeling like razor on skin
Vertical cutting in
But with water they fade
Darkness in the air
Twilight met concrete
Descends in silence
Blood stains on a pavement

Cola the Sith Lord of the Dark Side

If Cola was a Sith Lord, I would turn to the Dark Side
Like popping candy in my mouth
Feel the bubbles
Drink too much
Head south to the dunny
A runny mocha
You only rent your purchase
Taste sweet delight
Inspiration for the words
In the middle of the night

The Reaper Watches the Hour

A black bird
13th floor
Underneath the stars
Liquid illusion
Writer's confusion
Asymmetrical
Clock hits eleven
Death to come in the early hours of seven
Caped wing black gown
Skeleton reveals
A reaper scythes

Talked to Angels

As a baby
He cried in the cradle
Seeking love but only neglected
From the heroin mum injected
Now in a crib
Crying for the spoon
As an adult he's from foster homes
Soul sees the light
A spirit of peace
Walked the earth
Now deceased

The Diary of Belinda

Mama said
I'd be better off dead
She was fucked in the head
Scrubbed with steel wool and soap
While Daddy smoked dope
Drank instead
Melancholy
Tourniquet around the neck
How can she wind up in heck?
When her thoughts sometimes disconnect

The Mansion in the Sky

My spirit will fly
In a mansion in the sky
Resurrected from mortal death
Just a young man
Addicted to blood and roses
Watch the sunset goodbye
Never saw a sunset after he died
Blood of Christ returns
As all he's heroes burned
Solitude and darkness
He's only friend
Ashes that reborn
The devil respawned
Now the sun cast a shadow upon the man
Crumbled to ash
Returned to the land

The Satellite

The darkness slowly reappears
Planet earth once near
Now I orbit close to the sun
Off course…Navi computer down and it's cold and black

The sun propelled radiation and gamma light
Shell melting on sight
I've seen angels of heaven and seen the burning sun
What was once Cupid's arrow
Is shattering in fragments

Like an astronaut I
Float on a rope
But there's a hole in this sinking boat
The oxygen is leaking and the crew are comatose

Past planets I orbit in command
Will I see the stars of another man?
I enter a crab nebula and wormhole
In a black hole I have gain godly knowledge
Of the universe tonight

Holy Father

I pray to God
He puts me on call waiting
Is he on life support?
Cause he's not listening to my prayers
Surrounded by four walls
Caving in
How can he damn us for original sin?
How can you wash away life in a biblical flood?
Are you hearing me?
In heaven above

Stars

Up in the sky I dream of other worlds
In my little spaceship
Flying past the moon
Headed for a collision course
With the rockets
Satellites space stations
And pockets of gas clouds

A Cat's Life

Feed me now!
Obey my command!
Whiskers diet
Pondering life and the universe
While sleeping
Catch that string
I play
Claws sharp
Too cool to fetch a stick or a ball
Curious feet
Trip over owner
Was it on purpose?
Wakes up at 3 am want food
Will give you attention
When it's in the mood

A Dog's Life

Fetch
Lick saliva
Leave a present in the yard
Fire hydrants
Raise the leg
Farts that smell
Dog food not respectable
Why do you think
Dogs lick their testicles?
Bark
Roti meat
Small dogs with Napoleon complexes
Wipe their rear end on the carpet
Man's best friend

Memory

Struck in prime of life
Cruel illness erases time and mind
Just and empty soul
Never grow old
Can't understand
Her family are her loved ones
When she is told
Forgotten her life
Frustration anger discomfort
The dignity of this frail beautiful person
Vanquished
Left to sit in a nursing home
To slowly cruelly die
But still no euthanasia
We all ask
Why?

Projection of Time

Snowy New York
Light escapes through the cracks of the window
Curtain and holes in the roof
Projection still
Image
Prays for it to be real

The Wolf

Within a concrete forest
Trees concrete grey
Dab and cold
He howls
But no one listens today

You

Eyes shine right through to the soul
Smile melts the frost
Heart
An observatory to the stars
Lips like a radio telescope
Send messages
To Mars
By whispering in my ear
Sensations of intelligent life

No Rest on Earth

Exhausted
Death begins its eternal birth
Cannot stop those who die
Through bleakness of total death
Where misery does eternally rest
Beauty and peace wilt its final breath
And in the muddy fields
Soldiers lay
Poetic verse to rest in clay
I pray to stop these warring nations

Jupiter

Circling red storm
On a gas giant
Creator goes big and defiant
Beauty and gravity surround the globe
Peacefully
From Earth

Planet Earth

Outside this hemisphere
There's a planet which glows bright
Blue and white
Silent from its occupants
Ocular
Beautiful
Violent
Peaceful
Listening in space
Sending message out there for intelligent life
In space

Let There Be Light

Marching
To echoes of doom
Light born
When let there be light command
Oblivion of land
Radiation reigns
Mortal clay slain
Quiet earth
Ruins rot in time
No trace of mankind
Nuclear winter

The Day I Met God

Sitting on a hospital bed
God said
Hi I'm God, do you believe me?
I said yes

On the off chance that he was God I didn't want to piss
him off

The Mummy Returns

A guy on a bus
An awful fuss
Said he was a mummy
Smelt like he'd been alive for a thousand years

Seal Bay

Flapping
Flopping
Lifeless lumps
Sunbaking
On a windy day
Some swim out towards the horizon
Seal Bay

Silo Bunker

Vision of dying
Cold circular well
Swinging like an exhausted pendulum
Ruins
Silent still
Valves of ocean sweep across
Like a depressed albatross
Black bleak
Little light creeps

By the Light of the Fire

The dark from the moon
Solemn torment
He wrote
Which would bring his doom
Death came
The look in his eye
He dropped his pen
Heavy his heart did stop
Cold as a pebble
Mighty as a rock
Thrown in the sea
He summoned
To take him in the night

Blossom Does Decay

Blossom does decay
And surrounding life dies
All that life decays
And in death we try

To fight and disobey
The laws of physics
But to the curious morbid
Death is so exquisite

Descent of an Angel

Wings a blaze
Falling
Like a jet fighter
Heavy metal wings
Fly to the sun
Down by the gun
Smoking and twisting
In the air
Wine
Plummeting to Earth

Bombs Away

Wedged tale eagle
Dive
Glide in the clouds
Engine stealth
Radar
Not found
Soaring metres off the ground
Peace through fire power
A war dove

Lucid

Dream-like state
Fracture young minds
White light
Missile approach
Rewind
Wake up
Flamenco death rattle
Seen a skinny coffin
Weight of a former self
Death comes as a soldier
Weary and hungry

I Found My Words

I flew to the moon
Forgot about death
And all that doom
And through the darkness that lurks
Within my mind
My very own prison
Can't contain

She Walks in Battlefields

Empty
But the war
Rages on inside
Kinetic ability
Translucent being
Seen on the night
To those who have been seen
To those who inside scream
When you dream
You dream of her
A soldier's companion
A poppy for a ghost

The Darkest Soul

The darkest soul
Still shines
Still like the blues lake
The darkest soul can make you haunt and shiver
But in those
Rushes bullets
Of a suicide
Holds life of an innocence

Shadows

We choke
We smoke
Gas filled air
The toxification of life
Metal coffins
Go to work
Ticking down our toxic doom
Ice caps melt
Smog and pollution
Maybe extinction
Is our next evolution

Back to Earth

I'm floating in space
Radiation light
And no oxygen in sight
The darkness unforgiving
Off course and falling
Like a diving eagle hunting its pray
Headed for Earth
Life and death to humans
Oblivious in sleep
Earthling destructor
Carnivorous
Falling apart in the wings
Like a hand holding a hand grenade
Flame
Metal fragments
Light the sky

Five Minutes to Flatline

I'm gasping for air
Death is close
I'm hooked to a respirator
As I go comatose
I see the new world
It calls to me
From these tubes and machines
I want to be free
Hoping for death
But now I whimper
In a valley of death
Five minutes to flatline
Is all I have left

Creativity

I don't know
But the words are all that I've got
There's a vocabulary in my brain
That won't come out
So, I rhyme
So, I create
From a few words
Add death in the mix
And it seems to flow great
My next verse
Its time like Mary Shelley to reanimate
But I search for cure for the next verse
I lose my state
No more fixture on what I was thinking
I gravitate
To the vocabulary
Stuck in a cage
Open the thesaurus
The words write on the page
I've erased some keepers
Thinking they were crap
There ought to be a recycling box
For the brain
So, when you're thinking great you can go revisit

Tourniquet

Now her brain matches her mood
She fell from grace
Her eyes like mace
Found no beauty
In the human race
Tourniquet around her neck tightens
Tickling death in a dangerous foreplay
Her wings cut off with razors
Hugged in razor wire
She grazes
On Valium and sleepers
Levitating off the ground
The cross beam left with heavy burden
Makes a sound
Choir
Silence the birds like an earthquake stalking
Annabel gone from this world
Now she's talking to those who flirt with death
She kisses and takes their final breath
And God turns her into the angel of death

Behind the Curtain

I hear the audience behind the curtain
In a suit with a microphone
Adrenaline certain
The clock tick slows the fast
I want this very last minute to last
The curtains raised
I go out on the stage
The whole auditorium is clapping
I can hear them call out my name

Buried under Snow

She tried to stay
But this realm death is blind
The sorrow and hate for the man
In the last five minutes
Was her friend
And she swore she would haunt him until his very
End
Stab wounds on lily skin
Bloodstained snow
A serial murderer on the loose
The detectives too slow
But he will slip up
Until then
Pretty flowers in the snow

My Bleeding Affections

Your smile
Was like shattered glass
Embedded in to my heart
And I can't forget you
But remember my innocent crush
Maybe there was something there
But we both rushed
Now we go down different paths
I wonder if you were my deepest sorrow
My bleeding affections drain my life force from me
Soul
A photograph of you turned grey and faded and fragile in
the wind by the burning flame
Her bleeding affections
She can't contain

Hitchhiker

He walks these roads with a guitar
Where he's going is far
Thumb and arm stretched out like a deadly tentacle
Of an octopus
Mystical with glowing blue rings
Jewellery on his hand catches weary travellers' eyes
He picks him up
Speedometer and 140 kilometres
The hitchhiker plays his guitar
But it's a trancing tune
The driver clutches his chest
Car crashes
Hitting a tree
He gets out with his companion
Its quarter to three in the morning
They head for the light
The sirens muffled but growing from the distance
My family I'll miss them all
But the hitchhiker replies
You will see them all very soon

The Piano Woman

A man inside a bar lobby has been drinking for hours
He looks like a fried piece of turd
The barman slides him a drink
Pointing to the lady at the piano
She smiles
He drinks
Too many his thoughts are clouded
She's dressed in pink he no longer thinks
Pulls out a gun
Shoots her in the head
She falls to the ground in a pool of red
The crowd run around like disturbed ants
The barman slides him another drink
But he refuses
Cops come in their cuffing his wrist
No thanks I've just quit

Walk with Me into Bereavement

Here I am a figure of black
Weep no more
For I still the pain
With my scythe
Your sorrow is contained
Let me grieve for you
Let me hug the pain
Let me take your dying thoughts

The Crows Fall Silent by the Grave

They gather one by one
Tears fall
Like a nuclear winter
The fresh dirt cracks
Faint light from the sun

Her Time Has Come

The choir sings
Angels come
On this morning spring
Veil of white lace
Onto a tortured face
Here death resides
Spotlight on the stage of swan lake
Blood red exit wounds the vertical the horizontal
Shade of crimson
Shrouded in white cloth and lilies

The Haunting

Angry that I died
Angry deathly world
I don't reside
Flash of light
On a living entity
Levitating knife
Crack in the mirror
Séance
I draw nearer
Flickering light
Shadows on the wall grieve
Objects move
A wintry atmosphere

Under an Ecliptic Sky

Soldiers come out
Fireflies about
Under an ecliptic sky
Life that has died is reborn
Sanity is torn
Frayed ends worn
Soldiers' wives mourn
As a world unbelieved is born

Sun Shower

Rays of the sun
Droplets and a rainbow
As the clouds turn from grey to black
Water on my arms and face
Rays of the sun obliterate
The bleakest grey
Left with fresh rain smell for the day

Great Man

Read books on the porch
A nice fellow
Never put up with nonsense
Don't remember your voice
Perfect companion
A true hero

The Big Turd

I remember in Coffs Harbour with Nan and Pop
They took me to see the big turd
A fiberglass turd in someone's yard
With a dabble on the end of the tip
Had my photo taken to remember it

Darth Vader in Board Shorts

If Darth was a surfie
He could make the waves big
Be a regular on the beach
With his board and wax
His lightsaber, shorts and under dacks

Tim's Song

Midnight
No one hears me scream
No one sees my dreams
I think
Today's a good day to die

I don't know why
I feel so depressed
But life keeps dishing up a mess
I never thought
I'd take my life
But there's more happy
Memories
In this knife

The noose around my neck
Is the only thing
That's close to me
When oxygen stops my heart
Will I be free?

An Angry Sun

Fire
Floods
Temp rising
In heaven above
Mother Earth cries
Now the earth is burning
Dictators in command
Fire
Floods
Temperature rising
Angel of Death laughing
To kill on God's command

You Are the Perfect Drug

I need
When I see you
With other lovers
I bleed
As I look into your eyes
I knew it was time
To say goodbye
Red cascaded hair
Trapped eternally
In your stare

A Scotch for Dad

You weren't there
During the rough times
You treated us like an exhibition
But there were some good times

In a few years' time
We'll meet again
Hopefully then
Things will be different then
I never got to say goodbye
Spent some tears
To cry
Love you Dad
Here's a Scotch goodbye

Everybody Just Take a Cup of Calm the Fuck Down

Since Covid-19
We've been running around
Some breaking the law
Some panic buying
It's just toilet paper
Calm the hell down
Protests in the street
Masks litter the street
Science of the stupid

Batman Caused Covid-19

Batman's been in China
Now there's an outbreak of Covid-19
Batman died
It was a bio bomb from the Penguin
He's been outclassed
Robin just survived
On the skin of his arse
So now the world needs a new superhero
Maybe Spider-Man or the return of Jesus
But God help us
If anybody sneezes
We use to cough to cover a fart
Now we fart to hide a cough

Writer's Block 2

This is it
Take a chance
Like a razor to the vein romance
Write in the early hours
Write in my sleep
The dead poets I read still speak
Writer's block
Turning blue
A horrible shade
When nothing comes out new
Dream beautiful
Still waters run deep

Transformer's...Covid-19

Death is busy
He needs a breather
War in Europe
Don't understand that either
Batman gave us Covid
Now it's a transformer
Omicron
Vitamin BA virus

Stage fright

I'm on a stage
There's a light through the cracks
The audience is listening
There's no turning back
I touch the mic
I've got their attention
They're all mine
I type the words
They begin to flow
Look at the crowd below
I speak
The fear dissolves
These words trust in
I dearly hold

Death Was Screaming

I heard that death was screaming
I came to those hallowed halls
I saw the writing on the wall

Indiscriminate light and shadow
They took me too the gallows
And when the silence had gone
They thought something was wrong

I was there swimming on defiant
Dodging bullets becoming a giant
I swam in the clouds
And struck a thunderous cloud

He was so melancholic
And when the church bells sang
He morphed and grew fangs
He drew blood from the ashes
And the hallowed halls fell and crashes
And when he came right too
He was fitted with hospital tubes

He Drank a Red Bull to Give Him Wings

Silent lies the man
In a pool of blood
I think he tried to dive
It wasn't deep enough

Isn't Life Just Beautiful

There's a girl with suicidal thoughts
A home life that's like a tragedy played out
And as she downs the pills
Death gets a thrill and says
Isn't life just beautiful

Sending Messages out to Space

Wipe the tears off her face
Took some pills
Prayed for death
But if she closes her eyes
She may see loved ones past
Too late to die
Too late to live
Spectres fly above us

Battle

There's no sun in the sky
As angels mourn and cry
These black clouds don't strike lightning
Words brilliant
But fall short of a war

For Mabel and Bert

I dreamed of you the day you died
Can't forget the tears I cried
See a picture of both of you
And reminisce
Hope you now live in total bliss
From your loving grandson
A loving kiss

Memory

A beautiful mind
Struck in its prime
Cruel illness of time
Mind empty shell
To fatefully grow old in hell
Data delete
Children strangers

Every Cloud

Staring out the window wondering if things will be
the same
She looks in the mirror at the price of fame
People see her on the street
They want her signed name
She thinks…be careful what you wish for
She's sick of the game

Every cloud has a silver lining
Every cloud pours a little rain
Every cloud has a silver lining
'Cause when the sun comes out
You can feel great again

He drinking out the bottle
Anger knocks on the door
She fills her gun with lead after he throws her to the floor
Enough is enough she shoots him and then walks out the
door

Salem Winter Snow Storm

Persecution bleeds out the wrists of God
As ash, white falls upon the winter storm
Barbed wire for the youth
People marched like cattle to their death
A war machine keeps turning
Ash drifts through the towns

Invasion of the Plumber's Crack

I'm under attack
I'm under attack
From the invasion of the plumber's crack
Caught in the light
Caught in the trap
Grand CANYON size gap
I'm under attack
I'm under attack
From the invasion of the plumber's crack

Cottage Cheese

Regurgitator
Creamy like cheese
Liquid saliva
Ejected in the porcelain bowl
Carrots always there
White chunky bits
Smells like blue vein cheese
But not as nice
Like a cheesecake left in the sun
Dissolving in water

Agnetha

Beaten and left for dead
Never to sing again
She rides the subways
Goodbye to family and friends
Now distant
She roams at night
A subway hero
For all in danger

Cross her and she will tell you of your death
Complicated
Disconnected
A purple vigilante

Queen Lilith Black

She's haunted
Haunted by a vision of you
Walking the cemetery
Wondering
Bewildered
To enter
Light or dark
The orchestra play their tune
Dr yells clear
Cardiacs arrest
Respirator beeps
Lilith takes a breath
Suicide her comfort
Now her sorrowful hell
Too dark
Too light
Arms reach out
They call her name
Brain interrupted
Her world rearranged

A Reflection for the Bleak

Depressed
Life's a mess
He never thought he'd take his life
But there's more happy memories in this knife

The noose around his neck
The closest thing
When oxygen stops
His heart
And spirit free

Portrait in the Snow

She lies in the snow
Portrait of red and white
Decaying in the earth
Awakened in a séance
Whispers frosty in the early night
Seductress of decay
Loved ones' tears close by
Through the flickering flame
She in a coma

Dreaming of Packed Stadiums

Their screaming for me
My career is here
Drugs and alcohol
When the fame gets too much
Booking out stadiums
With long rock hair
And they can't get back
Cause they're already there
In heaven on a stage
And the crowd just stare

Funeral

And I stared into your cold black eyes
When you said goodbye
In time we will meet again
Maybe things will be different then
Never got to say goodbye

Stream of Consciousness

Nuclear arsenal begins
Sucking on a candy-coated Vicodin
Chewy caramel centre
You never went to
 The darkest place of an entertainer
In a container
Rose from the ashes
The spaceship crashes
Aliens on board smoke their stashes
Green little but mean
Eating beans
Then the smoke clears
It's filled my head
Alien probed
They're a little imbrued
Webbed feet
And ears pegged
Looking for DNA

Acoustic Black Hole

Sea cliff
Seduction
Razor and death
Sirens screeching
Singing on a treble clef
It seeks
Its breaths
No life
Funnel on the edge of a vacuumed
Acoustic black hole

The Milky Way

Curtain opens in the sky
Revealing stars and silver moons
Dust clouds and nebulas
Shooting stars
See eyes of creation
Through telescopes and irises
Astronomer below
Life kinetic flow
Cosmos grows
Giant suns
Eclipsed by monstrosities
Big Bang Theory remains defiant

Eulogy

I'm floating in the reaches of space
I look down on earth and see its beauty
Man's destruction like a giant fingerprint from space
My eulogy read out

I miss my loving family
But alas inspiration flows through me
The dark and light of space
And black holes surfacing
Dying stars
Are rebirthed

I fall towards Planet Earth
Pool of water
Hit by mortar
Living with reorder
Wake up refreshed
Arisen from death

The Bleeding Dove

Sounds of war light up the night
Call to arms, against enemy might
Repel the guns and missiles
With their hope for light
Nuclear warheads tick with delight
Jet fighters bomb apartments
Civilians rage
Take the place of the gun
On the world stage
Dangerous talk in a nuclear age
Blood and tears of loved ones
The bleeding dove

The Ocean

Mysterious ocean blood of
Adventurous skipping and pearls.
Shadowed deep loss with a
Glowing pool of water.
Home of sirens with different colours.
Look into the light and
Find the shell.

Whales

Whales
Are amazing creatures
They swim, dance, sing and play
With their fantastic blues and greys.
Calmly swimming in our oceans
Eating the smallest of shrimp
Growing 100 feet long
And breathe air just like us.
They're graceful and mysterious
In the deepest seas
Where no light can reach.
They sing through sonar, to their friends
Warra Whoosh
Up to the surface they spray from their spout
Like a living water fountain feature.
These gentle giants say hello
And show their calves to people on jetties and boats.
Their tails flap through the water
Like a splash and just float.
Submarines do not go as deep.
The largest animal on the planet
Majestic creature, the Antarctica blue whale
With the biggest of hearts.
Taken for granted
300,000 killed each year.
As land mammals, we pollute their habitat
Destroying the earth and seas.
Caught in fishing nets
And killed when harpoons are thrown
Bombs destroying their brains.
Are we a destructive plague?

When it comes to whales' peaceful minds.
Caught and sold on the black market
Killed for oil, blubber and cartilage
Their ribs used for corsets
For fashion curve shape.
Norway, Japan, Iceland, Greenland
Vs
Orca, Humpback, Beluga and Minke.

Flames

The crimson monster rose up
The trees creaked and ached
The plants gasped for air
The monster raged through the thicket
Consuming everything in its wake
Dragons awake with the fiery sun
Mother Nature's revenge has just begun
Climate change
A hot sun
A toddler tantrum out of control
The fire rages
Taking control

Trees in the Wind

Green giants swirling in the wind
Branches like human limbs
Oxygen for craving creative minds
They move like ballet dancers
Gracefully expressing on the world stage
Reincarnated as a poet's page

Swirling Sea

Like a hand rising
Blue
Filled with marine life
Ships rock to the rhythm of the beat of the water
An orchestra of water marine instruments
Playing a symphony
As the swirling seas crash into the shore
The audience applauds
Waves under the spell of the moon's gravity

Sea Shell

Mysterious ocean blood of adventurous skipping and
pearls
Shadowed deep loss with a glowing pool of water
Sunlight captures colours
An ornament
A necklace
Listen to the shell to your ear
Smooth and rough
Pearl white

Blistering Snowing Mountains

Giants of the land
Few have scaled their peaks
The snow peaks
Like an upside-down ice cream cone
The wind, low in oxygen at its viewing height
Reaching for the stars at night

Wandering Turtle

Under the moonlit sky
She glides and flops to the shore
Burying her eggs in the sand, a hard shell
For a wandering turtle, life can be hell
In the current, she surfs the Australian waters
Reaches a lifespan twice as long as us
While we remain oblivious to the perils of the deep
As the wandering turtle
Pops her head out to peep

Deep Abyss

There are mysterious sirens on the cliffs of the ocean
Calling travellers who have wandered too far.
With their beauty and grace, they can fool anyone
Who they call their lunch.
They seduce them, charm them, toy with them
And lead them down below, into the deep abyss they call
their home.
They blow them one final kiss before their life is about to
end.

Pretty Flowers in the Snow

Before I know my time is up
To become clay in the soil
For pretty flowers in the snow